Learn About Plants!

By
Steffi Cavell-Clarke

KidHaven
PUBLISHING

Published in 2018 by
KidHaven Publishing, an Imprint of Greenhaven Publishing, LLC
353 3rd Avenue
Suite 255
New York, NY 10010

Designer: Danielle Jones
Editor: Charlie Ogden

Cataloging-in-Publication Data

Names: Cavell-Clarke, Steffi.
Title: Leaves / Steffi Cavell-Clarke.
Description: New York : KidHaven Publishing, 2018. | Series: Learn about plants! | Includes index.
Identifiers: ISBN 9781534522466 (pbk.) | ISBN 9781534522428 (library bound) | ISBN 9781534522343 (6 pack) | ISBN 9781534522381 (ebook)
Subjects: LCSH: Leaves–Juvenile literature. | Leaves–Physiology–Juvenile literature.
Classification: LCC QK649.C38 2018 | DDC 581.4'8–dc23

Printed in the United States of America

CPSIA compliance information: Batch #BS17KL: For further information contact Greenhaven Publishing LLC, New York, New York at 1-844-317-7404.

Please visit our website, www.greenhavenpublishing.com. For a free color catalog of all our high-quality books, call toll free 1-844-317-7404 or fax 1-844-317-7405.

PHOTO CREDITS

Abbreviations: l–left, r–right, b–bottom, t–top, c–center, m–middle.

Front cover – alfocome, DPetlia Roman, Nik Merkulov, Kiselev Andrey Valerevich. 1 – italianestro. 2– Sunny studio. 4 – Romolo Tavani. 4br – GongTo. 5 main – amenic181. 5lm – Elena Elisseeva. 6 main – Jarous. 6cr – Ines Behrens–Kunkel. 7 main – sevenke. 7tl – vovan. 7ml – Carlos Caetano. 7bl – margaret tong. 8l – Fotofermer. 8ml – Kazakov Maksim. 8mr – LubaShi. 8r – JOAT. 9 main – Miao Liao. 9cl – Smileus. 10 main – Romolo Tavani. 10cr – rodimov. 11 main – alphaspirit. 11tl – Rock and Wasp. 11mr – TinnaPong. 11bl – Alexander Kalina. 12&13 – Dudarev Mikhail. 14 main – Thiraphut Anusakulroj. 14cr – Duct. 15 main – 88studio. 15t&ml – Smit. 15bl – TungCheung. 16 main – Szasz–Fabian Jozsef. 16cr – Africa Studio. 17 – adike. 18 main – Leah–Anne Thompson. 18cr – Kuttelvaserova Stuchelova. 19 – aleksandr hunta. 20 main – Aleksey Stemmer. 20cr – Ailisa. 21 mian – melis. 21tl – Alex Staroseltsev. 21bl – Kenneth Keifer. 22 main – Malivan_Iuliia. 22cr – Taiga. 23 – Nataliia Melnychuk.
Images are courtesy of Shutterstock.com, with thanks to Getty Images, Thinkstock Photo, and iStockphoto.

CONTENTS

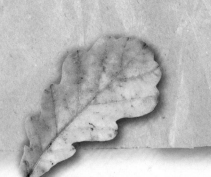

Words that look like **this** can be found in the glossary on page 24.

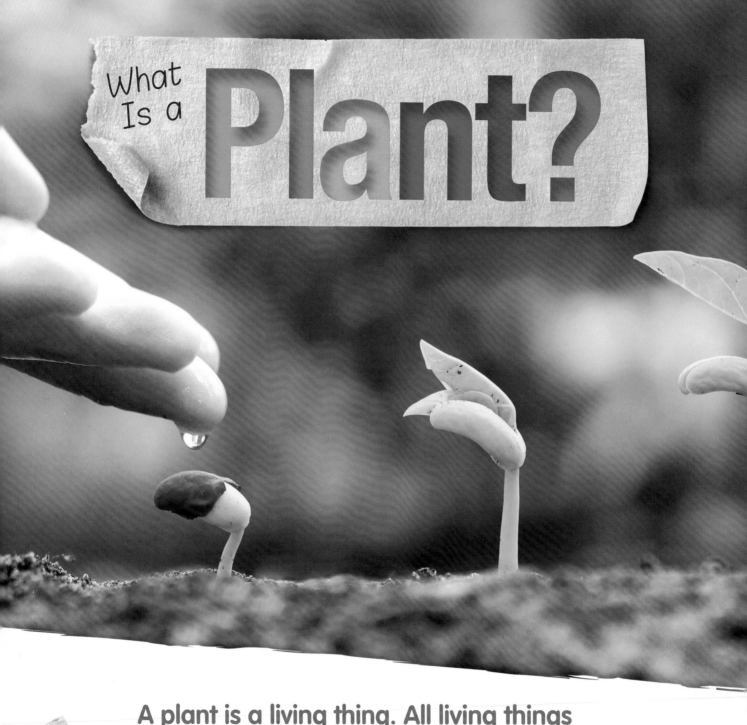

What Is a Plant?

A plant is a living thing. All living things need water, air, and **sunlight** to live.

There are many different kinds of plants. Most plants have roots, leaves, flowers, and a stem.

Plants live all around the world!

5

What Are Leaves?

Leaves are parts of a plant that grow from the stem.

Leaves have a very important job. They make food for plants!

What Do Leaves Look Like?

oval

round

needle

long

Leaves come in many different shapes and sizes.

Leaves are generally green, but some change color at different times of the year.

Many leaves turn brown or orange in fall.

9

How Do **Leaves** Grow?

As a plant grows, leaves will begin to grow from the stem.

The stem of a plant raises the leaves up toward the sun.

leaves

stem

11

Some trees lose their leaves during the fall and winter. These leaves change color and fall to the ground.

In the spring, the trees grow new leaves.

13

What Do **Leaves** Do?

The main job of a leaf is to make food for a plant.

Leaves **absorb** light from the sun and **gases** from the air around them.

Leaves need water to make food for
a plant. They get the water they need
from the roots.

16

The roots absorb water from the ground, which then moves up the stem and into the leaves.

leaves

The water is carried into the leaves.

stem

roots

17

Strange Leaves

The Venus flytrap is a meat-eating plant. When the plant feels an insect on its leaves, it snaps shut!

Stinging nettles have sharp hairs on their leaves. If you touch them, they can make your skin feel very itchy!

19

Leaves on Trees

deciduous trees

Forests are full of trees that have many leaves. Trees that lose their leaves during the fall and winter are called deciduous trees.

20

Evergreen trees do not lose their leaves during the fall and winter. Their leaves are often thin and spiky.

evergreen trees

21

Tasty Leaves

There are many leaves that people can eat. The leaves of lettuce and cabbage are very good for you.

Many animals eat leaves, too. Rabbits, giraffes, and koala bears all eat leaves.

23

GLOSSARY

absorb to soak up
forests areas of land covered in trees
gases invisible substances in the air
grow to naturally develop and increase in size
sunlight light from the sun

INDEX